The Sandcastles Program

Helping Children of Divorce Rebuild

Workbook
Ages 6-7

Pedmy Press

Other books in this series by M. Gary Neuman, LMHC

Sandcastles Workbook Ages 8-10
Sandcastles Workbook Ages 11-13
Sandcastles Workbook Ages 14-17

Books for parents by M. Gary Neuman
Helping Your Kids Cope With Divorce the Sandcastles Way

How to Make a Miracle: Finding Incredible Spirituality in Times of Happiness and Struggle

For more information visit: **www.mgaryneuman.com**

The Sandcastles Program: Helping Children of Divorce Rebuild

For further information, or to become a provider,
contact M. Gary Neuman at www.mgaryneuman.com

Published in the United States by
Pedmy Press

10 9 8 7 6 5 4 3 2 1

Name________________________________ Age _______ Boy / Girl

Welcome to the Sandcastles Program

This is your special workbook. You can use it to draw and create.

Draw a picture of your family when everyone lived together.

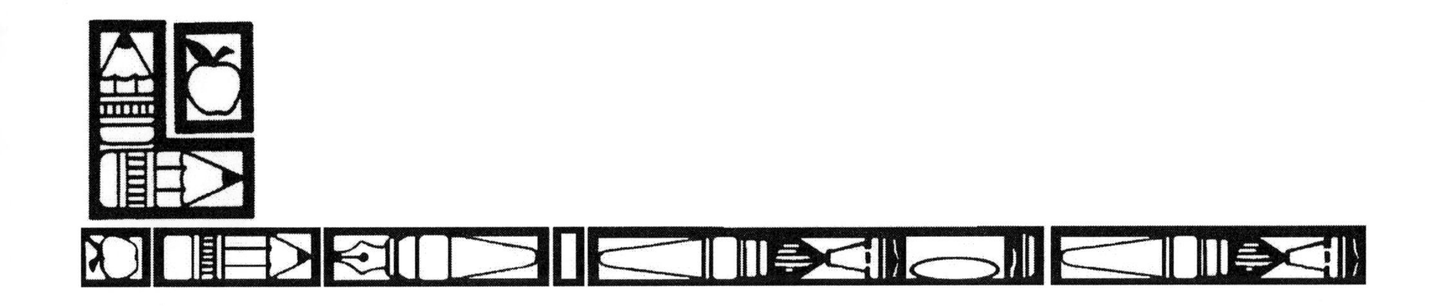

Notes to myself...

Draw a picture about your Mommy and Daddy not living together anymore.

My thoughts and feelings...

Write a letter to your Mommy and Daddy. What do you want to say to them about your family and about all of you not living together anymore?

Dear Mommy,

Dear Daddy,

Notes to myself...

Write a poem about your family.

Write a poem about divorce.

My thoughts and feelings...

Fill in the blanks.

I am happy when ______________________________

____

____

I am sad when ______________________________

____

____

I like ______________________________

I do not like ______________________________

When I think of my Mommy and Daddy not living together, I feel

____

____

____

Sometimes I dream about ______________________________

____

____

Notes to myself…

I am afraid that ____

____

I hope that ____

____

When I am older and have children I will ____________________

____

I do not understand ____

____

I cry when ____

____

I laugh when ____

____

My favorite thing in the whole world is ____________________

____

____

My thoughts and feelings...

Draw a picture of a genie.

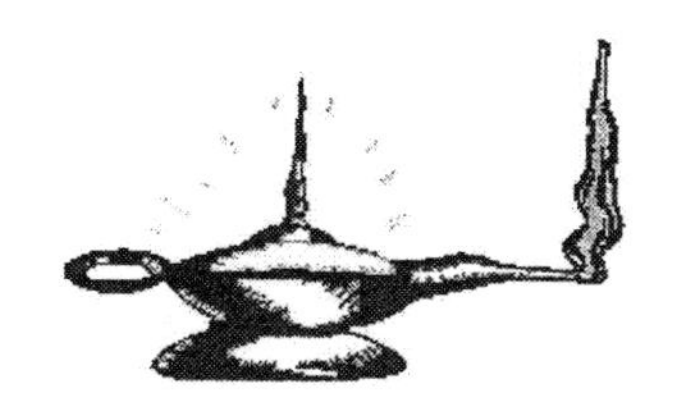

You have just freed the great genie from his lamp. He offers you three wishes. What would they be?

1.____

____

2.____

____

3.____

____

Notes to myself…

Use this page to create anything you want.
You could write a story about a family or draw a maze,
a cartoon, a fun game.

My thoughts and feelings...

When you are sad,
what are some things that you can do
to make yourself feel happy?

1. ____

____

2. ____

____

3. ____

____

4. ____

____

5. ____

____

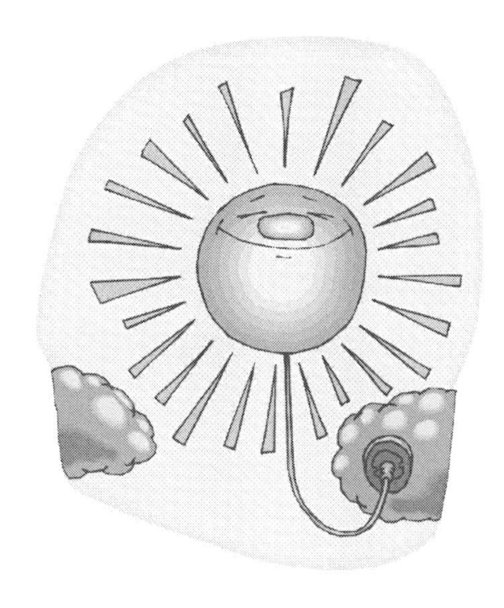

Notes to myself...

What questions would you like to ask your Mommy or Daddy?

1. ____

____

____

2. ____

____

____

3. ____

____

____

4. ____

____

____

5. ____

____

____

My thoughts and feelings...

Read the letter from Chad. Can you give him an answer?

Dear Gary,
I am 7 years old and I am in second grade. I have a dog and a bird. My mom and Dad got a divorce. What does that mean?

Chad

Dear Chad,
A divorce is when ________________________________

Some answers other people gave were:

A divorce is something grown-ups do. It means that parents won't be married anymore and will live in separate homes. Parents cannot divorce their children.

Notes to myself...

When going through a divorce, sometimes it helps to talk about it. Who are the people you can talk to? Draw pictures of them or write their names in the space below:

My thoughts and feelings...

People have a lot of different feelings:

How are you feeling right now?
Can you look at each face and think about something or some time that makes you feel that way?
Draw a face from your imagination and give it a feeling name.

Ask someone you love to draw a feeling face and tell you about their feelings.

Notes to myself...

Wish Upon A Star Cookies:

This is something you can do at home with a parent or grown-up friend.

YOU WILL NEED: $\frac{1}{2}$ teaspoon vanilla extract. 3 eggs, $2\frac{1}{2}$ cups of flour, 2 cups confectioners sugar (powdered), 1 cup butter or margarine (softened), 3 teaspoons baking powder.

Preheat oven to 350°. Lightly grease cookie sheets. In a large bowl, beat eggs. Add butter or margarine and vanilla. Gradually add flour, sugar, baking powder, and mix until well blended. Add more flour as needed to make a firm dough that isn't sticky, but be careful not to get it too dry.

Take a small piece of dough and press flat shape into a star or make faces using chocolate chips, coconut or sprinkles. Bake for 10 - 12 minutes or until lightly browned.

Talk about your wishes on the star cookies or talk about your feelings when you make the face cookies. When do you wear a happy smile? When are you sad or angry?

Let the cookies cool and enjoy!

My thoughts and feelings…

On this page are family puppets. Draw in the faces and cut them out. Tape or glue the people to a Popsicle stick or just hold them up in your hands. Think of a story about a family and have the puppets talk to each other.

MOMMY
Draw a MOMMY face

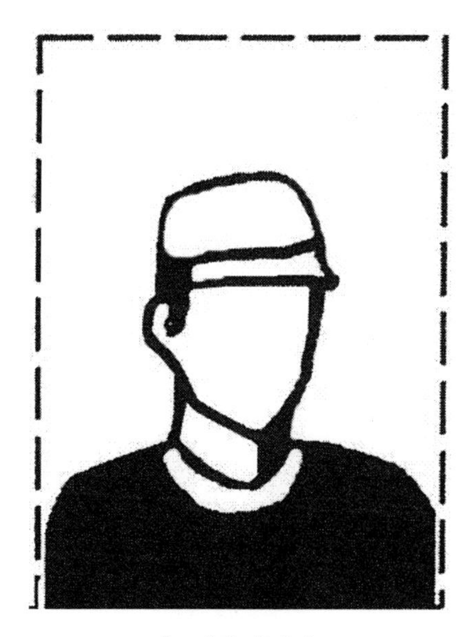

DADDY
Draw a DADDY face

BOY
Draw a BOY face

GIRL
Draw a GIRL face

Notes to myself…

Congratulations!!!

ON FINISHING THIS WORKBOOK

Remember how important it is
to share your feelings.

You can rebuild your own special

<u>SANDCASTLE</u>

If you are using this workbook in a Sandcastles group, please let us know how things went by checking the boxes below that apply.

Age________ Date_______ Location____________

	Yes	No	Not Sure
This program helped me understand more about separation/divorce.			
I learned that I can express my feelings.			
I learned other ways to handle problems that occur in my family.			
The program showed me that there is more than one way to be a family and it's okay to be different.			
I know that there are other children that share my feelings.			
I would recommend this program to other kids.			

More thoughts:

____

____

____

____

____

____

THANK YOU FOR YOUR ANSWERS.

Sandcastles Certificate

This certifies that

____

completed the Sandcastles Workbook/Program on

____